MW01193591

Table of Contents

Background to Common Reporting Standard

Tax evasion using offshore accounts has been a significant challenge to countries across the world. Exchange of information about offshore accounts across jurisdiction based on specific intelligence input has been assisting countries to address the issue, though partially. The Organisation for Economic Co-operation and Development (OECD) has been working with G20 countries to setup a framework for automatic exchange of information about offshore accounts based on certain accepted criteria.

The OECD together with G20 countries and in close cooperation with the EU and other stakeholders has developed the Standard for Automatic Exchange of Financial Account Information (AEFAOI), or the Standard. This is a standardised automatic exchange model, which has taken input from the Inter Governmental Agreement (IGA) designed under Foreign Account Tax Compliance Act (FATCA) to facilitate easy implementation at minimal cost.

The AEFAOI is also commonly referred to as The Common Reporting Standard ("CRS"). 55 Jurisdictions signed an agreement for CRS on 12 July 2015, with a commitment for reporting under CRS from 2017. 41 Countries have confirmed that they will initiate reporting from 2018. Within GCC, Saudi Arabia, Bahrain, Qatar, UAE and Kuwait have committed to adopt CRS and report from 2018.

CRS is based on Article 6 of the **Convention on Mutual Administrative Assistance in Tax Matters**. Key highlights of CRS are:

- Requires Model CAA agreement. The agreement is reciprocal and draws on the IGA approach for implementing FATCA. The agreement is arranged into sections. Key sections to refer to are:

    - Section 2: Type of information to be exchanged

    - Section 3: Time and manner of exchange

    - Section 5: Confidentiality and data safeguards

- Requires "standard systems" and "standard reporting template"

- Financial institutions includes custodial, depository and investment entities and specified insurance companies

- Identify reportable accounts using due diligence process (similar to FATCA requirements). Key factors to be considered while performing the due diligence are:

    - De minimis exemption does not exist for new and pre-existing accounts

    - Use of self certification for new individual accounts

    - Review of pre-existing accounts based on permanent residence address

    - Self certification for pre-existing accounts where conflicting evidence exist

- - Enhanced due diligence for higher value accounts including certification by Relationship Managers

- To be effective in stages starting 1 January 2016 for early adopters

- Annual reporting, starting 2017 for early adopters, and 2018 for others

- In UK and other European Union Countries, CRS is being implemented via European Directive on Administrative Cooperation (DAC)

- In addition to CRS, UK based entities are also exposed to Crown Dependencies and Overseas Territories (CDOT) reporting regime

- The International Tax Compliance Regulations 2015 that require UK Financial Institutions to identify, maintain and report information under CRS came into force on 15 April 2015

  - Being implemented using the "wider approach"

  - Identify the territory in which the account holder or controlling person is resident for income tax purposes

CRS timeline

CRS is effective starting 1 January 2016 for early adopters. Annual reporting requirements exist, starting 2017 for early adopters, and 2018 for others. The following diagram provides an overview of the key milestone under CRS:

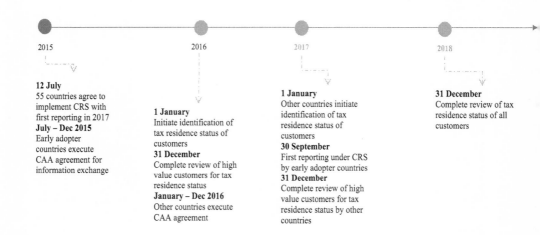

12 July
55 countries agree to implement CRS with first reporting in 2017
July – Dec 2015
Early adopter countries execute CAA agreement for information exchange

1 January
Initiate identification of tax residence status of customers
31 December
Complete review of high value customers for tax residence status
January – Dec 2016
Other countries execute CAA agreement

1 January
Other countries initiate identification of tax residence status of customers
30 September
First reporting under CRS by early adopter countries
31 December
Complete review of high value customers for tax residence status by other countries

31 December
Complete review of tax residence status of all customers

Why implement CRS?

- **CRS is Mandatory** in countries that have signed the CAA agreement

- As per the recent press release, G20 countries are considering "black listing" jurisdictions that do not comply with tax related information exchange

How do you know if CRS applies to you?

CRS applies to you if you are in a jurisdiction that has signed up to the Automatic Exchange of Information standard. The list of countries committed to CRS can be accessed using the following link:

https://www.oecd.org/tax/automatic-exchange/commitment-and-monitoring-process/AEOI-commitments.pdf

To know if you are in a jurisdiction that has committed to CRS and the date it applies to you, please access the above link.

As of 9 May 2016, 101 countries had committed to CRS. The following table provides an overview of the countries committed to AEOI and the timeline for reporting under the commitment for each of the jurisdiction:

JURISDICTIONS UNDERTAKING FIRST EXCHANGES BY 2017 (55)
Anguilla, Argentina, Barbados, Belgium, Bermuda, British Virgin Islands, Bulgaria, Cayman Islands, Colombia, Croatia, Curaçao, Cyprus, Czech Republic, Denmark, Dominica, Estonia, Faroe Islands, Finland, France, Germany, Gibraltar, Greece, Greenland, Guernsey, Hungary, Iceland, India, Ireland, Isle of Man, Italy, Jersey, Korea, Latvia, Liechtenstein, Lithuania, Luxembourg, Malta, Mexico, Montserrat, Netherlands, Niue, Norway, Poland, Portugal, Romania, San Marino, Seychelles, Slovak Republic, Slovenia, South Africa, Spain, Sweden, Trinidad and Tobago, Turks and Caicos Islands, United Kingdom

JURISDICTIONS UNDERTAKING FIRST EXCHANGES BY 2018 (46)
Albania, Andorra, Antigua and Barbuda, Aruba, Australia, Austria, The Bahamas, Bahrain, Belize, Brazil, Brunei Darussalam, Canada, Chile, China, Cook Islands, Costa Rica, Ghana, Grenada, Hong Kong (China), Indonesia, Israel, Japan, Kuwait, Lebanon, Marshall Islands, Macao (China), Malaysia, Mauritius, Monaco, Nauru, New Zealand, Panama, Qatar, Russia, Saint Kitts and Nevis, Samoa, Saint Lucia, Saint Vincent and the Grenadines, Saudi Arabia, Singapore, Sint Maarten, Switzerland, Turkey, United Arab Emirates, Uruguay, Vanuatu

Who are impacted by CRS

CRS applies to tax residents of a country maintaining financial assets abroad. It therefore impacts persons (both individuals and entities) that maintain financial assets outside their country of tax residence. In addition to the tax residents, it also impacts the following entities as they are required to implement appropriate infrastructure to support CRS:

- Governments
    - Tax authorities
    - Other regulatory bodies involved in tax related information exchange
- Financial Institutions – FIs:
    - Banks
    - Investment entities
    - Asset managers
    - Brokers
    - Insurance companies with life insurance (cash value) products
    - Credit card issuers
- Passive Non-Financial Foreign Entities (Passive NFFEs)
    - Investment groups
    - Family offices

Key requirements under CRS

Financial institutions are required to review their financial accounts and identify "reportable accounts". Reportable accounts are identified based on the "due diligence" performed using guidelines included in standard. Once identified, the reportable accounts are to be reported as per the requirements of the standard. The following diagram provides an overview of the key steps involved in CRS:

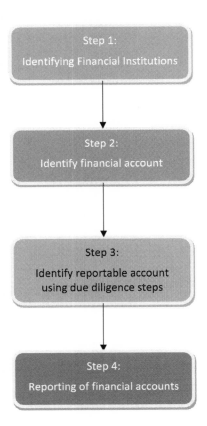

Registration

- Unlike FATCA, there is no central registration portal and issue of Global Intermediary Identification Number (GIIN) under FATCA

- However, Financial Institutions are required to register with the competent authorities of their home jurisdiction to perform reporting under CRS

Institutions considered as Reporting Financial Institution under CRS

The following entities are considered as Reporting Financial Institutions (FIs) under CRS:

- Banks

- Investment entities including

    o Asset manager

    o Mutual funds

    o Hedge fund

    o SPV, investment vehicles holding investments for a bank or FI

    o Brokers

    o Private equity entities

- Custodial entities

- Trusts

- Life insurance company with cash value insurance products

CRS also identifies the following entities as exempt from any due diligence and reporting requirements:

1. Government entities and their pension funds
2. International Organisations like the United Nations
3. Central Banks
4. Certain Retirement funds
5. Qualified Credit Card Issuers
6. Exempt Collective Investment Vehicles
7. Trustee documented trusts
8. Other low risk financial institutions

The following page provides the steps to be followed to identify whether you will be considered as a reporting FI under CRS.

Identifying a reporting FI under CRS

Only Financial Institutions identified as "reporting FI" are required to implement the due diligence process to identify reportable accounts and to comply with the reporting requirements under CRS. So how do we identify a reporting FI? The following diagram provides an overview of the key steps to be followed to validate whether you are a reporting FI under CRS:

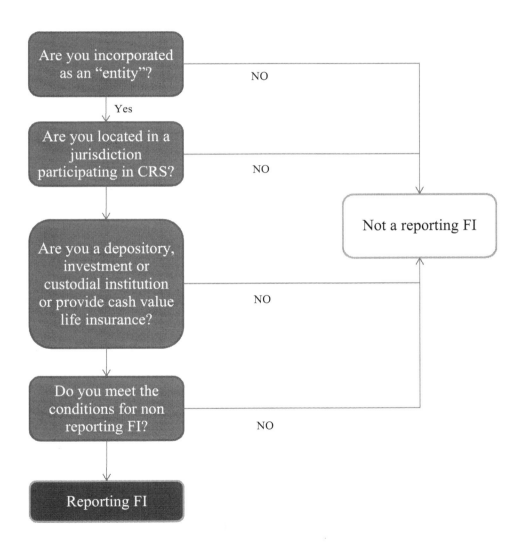

Financial Account under CRS

Reporting under CRS is applicable for "financial accounts" only. CRS identifies the following as Financial Accounts to which the regulations apply:

- Any depository account

    - Includes commercial, checking, savings, time, thrift account or any other account evidenced by a certificate of deposit or similar instrument

    - Amount held with insurance company under an agreement to pay interest

    - Credit balance in a credit card account

- Any custodial account

    - Account that holds any financial instrument or contract for investment for the benefit of another person

- Collaterals held by a bank

- Any equity or debt interest in the financial institution

- Any life insurance contract that include an investment component i.e.

    - Cash value life insurance contracts

    - Annuity life insurance contracts where the financial institutions are obliged to make some payments with respect to the contract irrespective of the life assured

A financial account will be reportable if:

1. The account is held by a person identified as a reportable person; or
2. The account is held by a passive non financial foreign entity with one or more controllable person who is a reportable person

Some accounts are also considered as non reportable. Account considered not reportable due to exemptions available under CRS includes:

1. Retirement and pension accounts
2. Non retirement tax favored accounts
3. Term life insurance contracts
4. Estate accounts
5. Escrow accounts

6. Depository accounts due to non returned overpayments
7. Other low risk excluded accounts as specified by each of the local jurisdictions

Due diligence requirements under CRS

Chapter 4 of CRS defines the rules for applying due diligence. Due diligence requirements are divided into those related to new accounts and those related to pre existing accounts.

Every jurisdiction participating in CRS is required to define the date from which the rules for due diligence need to be applied for new accounts. Any person opening a financial account after the specified date will be required to provide additional information to the participating FIs to assist in identifying the customer's tax residency status.

Due diligence requirements for new customers

Financial Institutions should follow the following steps to identify the tax residency status of new customers:

- Due diligence requirements exist both for individuals and entities

- Due diligence requirements similar to FATCA and is based on "self certification" by customers

- Sample self certification forms are published by OECD. These have been used by various jurisdictions to design their own self certification forms. We have seen examples where jurisdictions have combined the self assessment forms for FATCA and CRS. The following links can be used to access the self certification forms published by various jurisdictions and the standard published by OECD

    - Entity tax residency self certification form from OECD (http://www.oecd.org/tax/automatic-exchange/crs-implementation-and-assistance/BIAC-CRS-ENTITIES-Self-Cert-Form.pdf)

    - Individual tax residency self certification form from OECD (http://www.oecd.org/tax/automatic-exchange/crs-implementation-and-assistance/BIAC-CRS-INDIVIDUAL-Self-Cert-Form.pdf)

- Customers are required to identify their tax residence status and list all countries where they are tax resident

- FIs are required to verify the information against information collected as part of the AML/KYC process

- The International Tax Compliance Regulations 2015 that require UK Financial Institutions to identify, maintain and report information under CRS came into force on 15 April 2015

    - Being implemented using the "wider approach"

    - Identify the territory in which the account holder or controlling person is resident for income tax purposes

Due Diligence requirements - Pre existing accounts

Pre existing accounts are accounts opened before the date on which CRS becomes effective in any jurisdiction. CRS allows Reporting FIs to classify the financial accounts opened before the effective date into the following buckets:

1. High value accounts: Financial Accounts with balance above US$ 1 million
2. Low value accounts: Financial Account below US$ 1million
3. De minimis accounts: Financial Accounts maintained by entities that are below US$ 250,000 are identified as accounts below de minimis threshold. FIs can consider these accounts as non reportable without performing any review.

Note: De minimis threshold is not available for individual accounts.

Due diligence requirements for pre existing accounts:

- Accounts with balance above US$ 1 million is identified as "High Value" accounts

    - Review electronic data available about the customer in the IT systems of the FI. Identify if the customer has tax residency in any participating country. If yes, the account is identified as a reportable account. Self assessment for CRS should be obtained from the customer.

        o For Passive NFFE, the tax residency status of the controlling person will need to be identified and if such persons have tax residency in other jurisdiction, the entity will be identified as a reportable account

    - If self certification has been obtained from the customer, identify if the customer has tax residency in any participating country. If yes, the account is identified as a reportable account

        o For Passive NFFE, the tax residency status of the controlling person will need to be identified and if such persons have tax residency in other jurisdiction, the entity will be identified as a reportable account

    - If a review has been performed based on publically available information, identify if the customer has tax residency in any participating country. If yes, the account is identified as a reportable account

        o For Passive NFFE, the tax residency status of the controlling person will need to be identified and if such persons have tax residency in other jurisdiction, the entity will be identified as a reportable account

- Perform enhanced due diligence including review of customer files. Identify if the customer has tax residency in any participating country. If yes, the account is identified as a reportable account

  - o For Passive NFFE, the tax residency status of the controlling person will need to be identified and if such persons have tax residency in other jurisdiction, the entity will be identified as a reportable account

- *For early adopters, high value account reviews should be completed by 31 December 2016*

- Accounts with balance below US$ 1 million is identified as "Low Value" accounts

  - Only electronic data search required for low value accounts

  - *Low value accounts have to be reviewed as per the guidance issued in each of the jurisdiction, ideally before the end of 2018*

- *De minimis value of US$ 250,000 exists for entities*

- *No De minimis value exists for individuals i.e. all individual accounts need to be reviewed*

What will be reported under CRS?

- Information about reportable person (individuals) Passive NFFE with controlling person in the reporting jurisdiction for an Entity

    - Name

    - Address

    - Jurisdiction of residence

    - Tax Identification Number (TIN)

    - Date of Birth

    - Place of Birth

    - The account number

    - The account balance or value of the account held by the NFFE

    - Name and identification number of reporting financial institution

    - Gross amount of interest, gross amount of dividend or other income and the gross proceeds from the sale or redemption of property paid or credited to the custodial account

    - Total amount of gross interest paid or credited to the depository account during the calendar year

    - The total gross amount paid or credited to the account including the aggregate amount of redemption payments made to the Account Holder during the calendar year or other appropriate reporting period.

How to report?

- CRS report need to be submitted using the XML schema published as part of the CRS regulations

- CRS report to be submitted to the local competent authority

- Competent authority to share reports with other jurisdictions

Key steps to implement CRS – at the country level

OECD has prescribed four steps to implement CRS in any country:

- **Step 1**: Implementing domestic law including defining the regulations and issues guidance for Common Reporting Standard taking into consideration the AEOI standard setup by OECD

- **Step2**: Selecting a legal basis for automatic exchange of information under CRS

- **Step 3**: Implementing Information Technology (IT) and administrative infrastructure for CRS. Countries will also be required to mobilize appropriate resources to support the initiative

- **Step 4**: Implementing safeguards for protecting confidentiality, integrity and availability of data

Key steps to implement CRS – at the financial institution level

The following diagram provides an overview of the key steps to be undertaken by a Financial Institution to implement CRS:

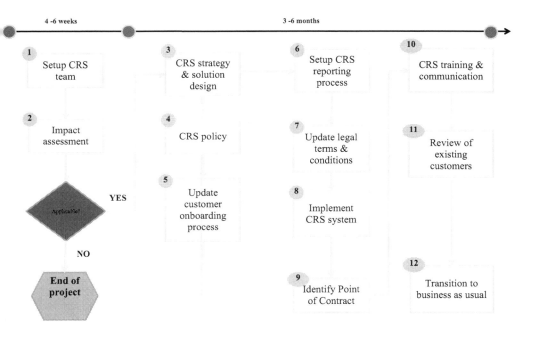

Key risks and challenges

Implementing CRS presents significant risks and challenges to financial institutions across the world. Some of the key issues being faced by institutions include:

1. **Lack of knowledge to define tax residence status:** Customers are generally not well versed with factors that will define tax residency status in a country. As CRS requires customers to self declare their tax residency status, the information provided by customers may not be very accurate

2. **Difficulty to validate the information provided by the customer:** Tax residency status is not defined in the documents provided by customers at the time of establishing a relationship to open financial accounts. Therefore, it is difficult for banks and other financial institutions to verify the information shared by customers

3. **Lack of de-minimis rule for pre existing individual accounts:** This will mean institutions will have to review all individual accounts without any exception. This may take additional effort and resources

4. **Training and awareness:** As requirements related to tax residency status is not widely known, appropriate training and awareness effort will be required to make CRS compliance effective

5. **Lack of penal clauses:** Unlike FATCA, CRS does not provide for withholding or similar penal clauses. This may make it difficult to ensure full compliance by all participating FIs

Summary

- Common Reporting Standard is the new standard for tax related information exchange

- Requires Financial Institutions to implement updates to their customer identification process

  o Based on residency status of customers

  o Driven by self certification

  o Early adopters to apply new customer identification process from 1 January 2016, other signatories from 1 January 2017

- First reporting under CRS in 2017 for early adopters. Reporting using standard XML format (similar to FATCA)

- No withholding requirements exists

- May require changes to processes, IT systems, forms, legal terms and conditions

- Requires a transformation process including training and awareness across the FI

- FIs can benefit from FATCA related processes, systems implemented for minimizing effort for CRS implementation

Glossary

Term	Explanation
AEOI	Automatic Exchange of Information
Active NFFE	An active NFFE (non-financial foreign entity) is any entity that is a NFFE if 1. Less than 50 percent of its gross income for the preceding calendar year is passive income and 2. Less than 50 percent of the weighted average percentage of assets (tested quarterly) held by it are assets that produce or are held for the production of passive income (i.e. dividends, interest, annuities etc.)
Competent Authority	The entity responsible for CRS in the jurisdiction
Controlling Persons	The natural persons who exercise control over an entity. In the case of a trust, such term means the settlor, the trustees, the protector (if any), the beneficiaries or class of beneficiaries, and any other natural person exercising ultimate effective control over the trust, and in the case of a legal arrangement other than a trust, such term means persons in equivalent or similar positions. The term "Controlling Persons" shall be interpreted in a manner consistent with the Recommendations of the Financial Action Task Force.
Custodial Account	An account (other than an Insurance Contract or Annuity Contract) for the benefit of another person that holds any financial instrument or contract held for investment (including, but not limited to, a share or stock in a corporation, a note, bond, debenture, or other evidence of indebtedness, a currency or commodity transaction, a credit default swap, a swap based upon a nonfinancial index, a notional principal contract, an Insurance Contract or Annuity Contract, and any option or other derivative instrument).
Custodial Institution	Any entity that holds, as a substantial portion of its business, financial assets for the account of others. An entity holds financial assets for the account of others as a substantial portion of its business if the entity's gross income attributable to the holding of financial assets and related financial services equals or exceeds 20 percent of the entity's gross income during the shorter of: 1. The three-year period that ends on December 31 (or the final

Term	Explanation
	day of a non-calendar year accounting period) prior to the year in which the determination is being made; or 2. The period during which the entity has been in existence.
Depository Account	Includes any commercial, checking, savings, time, or thrift account, or an account that is evidenced by a certificate of deposit, thrift certificate, investment certificate, certificate of indebtedness, or other similar instrument maintained by a Financial Institution in the ordinary course of a banking or similar business. A Depository Account also generally includes an amount held by an insurance company under an agreement to pay or credit interest thereon.
Depository Institution	Any entity that accepts deposits in the ordinary course of a banking or similar business.
Entity	A legal person or a legal arrangement such as a trust.
FI	Financial Institution. CRS identifies any financial institution outside as a FI
Financial Account	An account maintained by a Financial Institution, and includes: 1. In the case of an entity that is a Financial Institution solely because it is an Investment Entity, any equity or debt interest (other than interests that are regularly traded on an established securities market) in the Financial Institution; 2. In the case of a Financial Institution not described in subparagraph 1(s)(1) above, any equity or debt interest in the Financial Institution (other than interests that are regularly traded on an established securities market), if • The class of interests was established with a purpose of avoiding reporting in accordance with this Agreement; and 3. Any Cash Value Insurance Contract and any Annuity Contract issued or maintained by a Financial Institution, other than a noninvestment-linked, nontransferable immediate life annuity that is issued to an individual and monetizes a pension or disability benefit provided under an account, product, or arrangement identified as excluded from the definition of Financial Account in Annex II. Notwithstanding the foregoing, the term "Financial Account" does not include any account, product, or arrangement identified as excluded from the definition of Financial Account in Annex II.

Term	Explanation
Financial Institution	Custodial Institution, a Depository Institution, an Investment Entity, or a Specified Insurance Company.
CAA	CRS requires countries to execute a Model Competent Authority Agreement ("CAA") providing the international legal framework for the automatic exchange of CRS information.
First Model CAA	The first Model CAA -is a bilateral and reciprocal model. It is designed to be used in conjunction with Article 26 of the OECD Model Double Tax Agreement.
Second Model CAA	The second Model CAA -is a multilateral CAA that could be used to reduce the costs of signing multiple bilateral agreements (although the actual information exchange would still be on a bilateral basis). This could be used in conjunction with the Convention, something a very significant number of jurisdictions have already done.
Third Model CAA	The third Model CAA -is a non-reciprocal model provided for use where appropriate (e.g., where a jurisdiction does not have an income tax).
Investment Entity	Any entity that conducts as a business (or is managed by an entity that conducts as a business) one or more of the following activities or operations for or on behalf of a customer: 1. Trading in money market instruments (cheques, bills, certificates of deposit, derivatives, etc.); foreign exchange; exchange, interest rate and index instruments; transferable securities; or commodity futures trading; 2. Individual and collective portfolio management; or 3. Otherwise investing, administering, or managing funds or money on behalf of other persons.
MoF	The Ministry of Finance (MoF) is responsible for formulating and implementing the financial policies of the Kingdom of Bahrain within the overall vision of the Bahrain Government.
OECD	Organisation for Economic Cooperation and Development
Passive NFFE	The term passive NFFE means an NFFE other than an excepted and active NFFE.
Preexisting Account	A Financial Account maintained by a Reporting Financial Institution as of December 31, 2016.
Reporting FI	Financial institutions that are located in a jurisdiction that has participated in the CRS program

Made in the USA
Middletown, DE
06 October 2023

40337712R00017

....